Jerry Seinfeld

JERRY SEINFELD
BIOGRAPHY

A Life In Laughter

Bobby T. Leddy

Jerry Seinfeld

All rights reserved. No part of this publication may be reproduced, distributed, or transmitted in any form or by any means, including photocopying, recording, or other electronic or mechanical methods, without the prior written permission of the publisher, except in the case of brief quotations embodied in critical review and certain other noncommercial uses permitted by copyright law.

Copyright © Bobby T. Leddy 2024

Jerry Seinfeld

TABLE OF CONTENTS

INTRODUCTION

CHAPTER 1: WHO IS JERRY SEINFELD

    1.1 Early Years

    1.2 Childhood Influence

    1.3 Discovering A Passion For Comedy

CHAPTER 2: COMEDY JOURNEY BEGINNINGS

    2.1 From Open Mic To Stardom

    2.2 Comedy Clubs And The New York City Scene

    2.3 Rise To Prominence

CHAPTER 3: THE SHOW ABOUT NOTHING

    3.1 Establishing A Cultural Phenomenon.

    3.2 Behind The Scenes Of The Iconic Sitcom.

CHAPTER 4: BEYOND SEINFELD

    4.1 Exploring New Frontiers

    4.2 Post-seinfeld Projects And Endeavors

    4.3 Challenges In The World Of Entertainment.

Jerry Seinfeld

        4.4 Triumphs In The Entertainment Field
CHAPTER 5: PERSONAL LIFE
        5.1 Personal Milestones
        5.2 Managing the balance between public recognition and personal space.
CHAPTER 6: LEGACY
        6.1 Impact On Comedy
        6.2 Influence On Modern-day Comedians
        6.3 Long-lasting Popularity And Significance In Culture
CONCLUSION

Jerry Seinfeld

INTRODUCTION

In the busy center of Brooklyn, surrounded by the noise of daily life, a young boy named Jerry Seinfeld found something remarkable: the deep impact of humor. Right from the beginning, his life appeared to be in tune with the comedic timing, almost as if destiny had planned his path to become a part of comedy history.

Imagine a young Jerry, with his messy hair and a strong curiosity for the oddities of life. When he made his first joke, it was clear that he had a unique talent - the skill to find humor in everyday things and elevate the ordinary with his quick wit.

Jerry's talent for comedy blossomed as he maneuvered through the confusing passages of his teenage years. His comedic skills improved through late-night brainstorming sessions and spontaneous performances at family events. Every joke he told acted as a clue on the journey that eventually brought him to the iconic stages

Jerry Seinfeld

of New York City, where aspirations are transformed under the bright lights and enthusiastic cheers.

Jerry encountered obstacles and mishaps along the way. His rapid ascent to fame was accompanied by setbacks such as rejection letters, overlooked chances, and even audience members who heckled him. Nevertheless, Jerry persevered in his quest for the perfect punchline, driven by a strong faith in the ability of laughter to bring about positive change.

Seinfeld arrived suddenly and changed the direction of comedy forever, like a flash of light in the dark sky. It was a sitcom with no specific theme, which led Jerry to become a highly successful television star.
Through each episode, he uncovered the quirks of modern life with great accuracy and charm.

Jerry's narrative goes beyond Studio 8H. It's about bouncing back and adapting to the unpredictable nature of fame and fortune with dignity. It's a blend of humor

Jerry Seinfeld

and moments of reflection, creating a complex and compelling story.

Come along with me, my dear reader, as we explore the remarkable life of Jerry Seinfeld - a life characterized by humor, intelligence, and a contagious zest for life that never fails to captivate and entertain viewers worldwide.

Jerry Seinfeld

CHAPTER 1: WHO IS JERRY SEINFELD

Jerry Seinfeld is a highly accomplished and prominent comedian, actor, writer, producer, and director in America. He gained fame as the co-creator, executive producer, and lead actor of the acclaimed television series Seinfeld, which aired on NBC for nine seasons from 1989 to 1998.

The television series Seinfeld was famously described as a "show about nothing" because it focused on the ordinary lives of four unmarried friends in New York City. Jerry Seinfeld played a fictionalized character based on himself, with Jason Alexander, Julia Louis-Dreyfus, and Michael Richards portraying his friends. The show's sarcastic humor and focus on mundane details of daily life struck a chord with viewers.

Before Seinfeld, Jerry had risen through the ranks of the stand-up comedy scene in New York City after making

Jerry Seinfeld

his debut at an open mic night in 1976. His unique comedic style and outlook on ordinary life received high praise. He made frequent appearances on late-night talk shows and had a comedy special on HBO before developing Seinfeld.

After the show ended in 1998, it gained popularity through syndication and built a larger fan base. Jerry Seinfeld has been actively touring for stand-up comedy, worked on projects such as the documentary Comedian, and created the web series Comedians in Cars Getting Coffee. With a current estimated net worth exceeding $900 million, he is regarded as one of the most accomplished and influential comedians ever.

1.1 Early Years

Jerry Seinfeld, born on April 29, 1954, in Brooklyn, New York, grew up in the suburb of Massapequa, Long Island. His father, Kalman, worked as a sign maker, and his mother, Betty, was a homemaker.

Jerry Seinfeld

Jerry experienced a fairly standard middle-class childhood during the 1960s. He went to East Lake Elementary School and later enrolled at Massapequa High School as a child. His passion for comedy started at a young age, and he would often amuse his friends with humorous impressions and jokes.

Jerry completed his high school education in 1972 before enrolling in a communications and theater program at Queens College in New York. He completed his degree in 1976 and dedicated more time to his stand-up comedy career while studying at Queens College.

In 1976, he got his first big opportunity when a scout noticed him at a New York City club called Catch a Rising Star. This eventually resulted in him being featured on an HBO special hosted by Rodney Dangerfield in the same year. Following that, Jerry started appearing on popular TV programs such as The Tonight Show hosted by Johnny Carson in 1981.

Jerry Seinfeld

In the early years, Jerry honed his comedic skills by performing at open mic nights, working in comedy clubs, and gaining exposure on late-night TV. These experiences were essential in helping him develop his unique observational style, which ultimately led to the massive success of Seinfeld in the 1990s.

1.2 Childhood Influence

Jerry attributes his sense of humor to his family's dynamics during his upbringing. He recalls that his parents had a loving but dysfunctional relationship that inspired his comedic material. His mother was outspoken and loud, while his father was passive and quiet, leading to a contrasting parental dynamic that influenced Jerry's perspective on relationships and human behavior.

Growing up in a Jewish household on Long Island greatly influenced Seinfeld's comedic perspective. The emphasis within Jewish culture on communication, debate, and challenging authority provided Jerry with a

Jerry Seinfeld

foundation for his observational and questioning comedic approach, which delves into the details of everyday experiences.

Jerry's upbringing in the New York City area allowed him to be surrounded by a variety of individuals, mindsets, and comedic inspirations that influenced his urban style of humor. The quick-witted and straightforward communication style of New Yorkers greatly impacted his way of delivering jokes and his ability to find humor in every situation.

From a young age, Jerry showed a talent for noticing the peculiarities, inconsistencies, and comical aspects of human behavior and contemporary society. This sharp observation of the absurd in the ordinary activities of everyday life formed the foundation of his renowned observational humor.

Jerry's childhood was not explicitly tragic, but it involved a combination of Jewish cultural humor, dysfunctional family relationships, and exposure to the

Jerry Seinfeld

diverse environment of New York City, which ultimately helped shape his unique comedic style.

1.3 Discovering A Passion For Comedy

During his time at Queens College in the early 1970s, Jerry Seinfeld started to hone his comedic skills. He became a member of the school's Blazing Chips comedy group and regularly entertained at the college's coffee shop.

Jerry was able to focus on developing funny material, improving his on-stage charisma, and becoming more at ease when performing in front of live crowds. He discovered that he had a talent for observational comedy that connected with audiences at colleges.

During his time in college, Jerry expanded beyond just Queens College and began exploring open mic nights and comedy clubs throughout the New York City area. Establishments such as Catch a Rising Star and The

Jerry Seinfeld

Improv provided him with essential stage time to continue improving his comedic routine.

While still a student at Queens College in the mid-1970s, he served as the emcee at Budd Friedman's iconic club The Improv. This experience allowed the aspiring comedian to be fully involved in the vibrant New York City comedy scene.

Comedic Inspirations: At that time, Jerry was highly influenced by observational comedians such as Robert Klein and Bill Cosby. He was impressed by their talent for finding humor in everyday situations and observations. This motivated Jerry to create his style of reflective, conversational comedy.

Early exposure to television: Jerry started receiving some early TV exposure in the mid-1970s by regularly performing at clubs around New York during college. He appeared on television shows such as ABC's Sammy Part VI in 1976 and a Rodney Dangerfield HBO special

Jerry Seinfeld

in 1976. This increased his comedic aspirations after finishing college.

During his college years, Jerry, a young comedian in his late teens and early 20s, was able to explore his passion for comedy and improve his skills, paving the way for his future success in the entertainment industry.

Jerry Seinfeld

CHAPTER 2: COMEDY JOURNEY BEGINNINGS

Upon completing his studies at Queens College in 1976, Jerry had his big break when he was selected to participate in a Rodney Dangerfield HBO special, which provided exposure to a wider audience for the 22-year-old entertainer.

Jerry relocated to Manhattan to be near the vibrant comedy scene in New York City. After finishing college, he decided to live in a compact one-bedroom apartment on the Upper West Side. Jerry spent numerous evenings in Greenwich Village honing his material at comedy clubs.

In 1977, Jerry made his debut at The Comedy Store located in Los Angeles. This iconic venue served as a starting point for numerous upcoming celebrities. Mitzi Shore, the owner, started guiding Jerry and providing

Jerry Seinfeld

him with opportunities to try out fresh material there regularly.

Road Shows: In the late 1970s, Jerry started traveling and performing at comedy clubs throughout the United States and Canada. This allowed him to continue developing his material, improving his performance, and attracting fans outside of New York City.

In 1981, Jerry achieved a significant accomplishment by appearing on The Tonight Show Starring Johnny Carson for the first time. This was seen as a great opportunity for emerging comedians to gain visibility on a well-known program.

In the early 1980s, Jerry started to receive greater recognition for his distinctive conversational style and relatable observational humor. He made frequent appearances on Late Night with David Letterman and headlined an HBO special in 1981.

Jerry Seinfeld

The road to success may appear sudden, but in reality, it is built on years of dedication and hard work. The initial years after completing college spent carefully planning and navigating the comedy scene, played a vital role in setting the stage for Seinfeld's rapid ascent to stardom in the following decade.

2.1 From Open Mic To Stardom

Jerry began his comedy career performing at open mics and small clubs in New York before hitting the road extensively in the late 1970s. He toured throughout the United States and Canada, making appearances at numerous comedy clubs along the way.

He was able to gain valuable experience performing on stage, where he could develop new material and refine his distinctive observational style in front of varied audiences every night. Iconic venues such as The Comedy Store in Los Angeles and Catch a Rising Star in New York City were where he frequently performed.

Jerry Seinfeld

Television Appearances: Seinfeld gained significant visibility on television in the late 1970s by appearing on programs such as ABC's Sammy Part VI in 1976. However, it was his stand-up performance in 1981 on The Tonight Show Starring Johnny Carson that ultimately led to his breakthrough.

As Seinfeld's fame increased, he made more prominent appearances on popular shows like Late Night with David Letterman in the early 80s. His comedy was brought to a national audience through a 1981 HBO special.

Growing popularity: Although he didn't become famous overnight, Seinfeld worked hard to establish his reputation by touring consistently and appearing on television during the 1980s. His unique conversational approach, New York flair, and skill at humorously breaking down ordinary topics helped him attract an increasing number of supporters."

Jerry Seinfeld

In the late 1980s, Seinfeld was known as one of the most popular comedians in the United States. His widespread popularity led to the creation of his own NBC television show, which debuted in 1989 and aired for 9 memorable seasons until 1998.

Jerry Seinfeld rose to superstardom and solidified his reputation as a top comedian of his time thanks to the huge success of his show Seinfeld. However, it was his years of hard work on stage that paved the way for him to achieve such great success.

2.2 Comedy Clubs And The New York City Scene

Seinfeld's development was greatly influenced by his frequent performances at the legendary Comedy Cellar in Greenwich Village, Manhattan, during the late 1970s. This underground club provided an intimate setting for him to work on new material.

Jerry Seinfeld

Manny Dworman, the owner, created a nurturing space at the Cellar for up-and-coming comedians such as Jerry to develop their unique style. The Cellar's authentic and unfiltered ambiance proved to be an ideal breeding ground for Seinfeld's satirical and observant comedy.

Discover a Rising Star: Catch a Rising Star, a popular New York establishment where Seinfeld performed in his early days, is located on the Upper East Side. It was at this venue in 1976 that Jerry caught the attention of a talent scout, ultimately leading to his appearances on television shows such as Rodney Dangerfield specials."

Catch a Rising Star's exhibitions served as a platform for aspiring comedians to gain visibility in front of potential agents, television producers, and other influential individuals who could potentially launch their careers."

As a student at Queens College, Seinfeld often served as the host at Budd Friedman's influential Improv club in

Jerry Seinfeld

Manhattan during the mid-1970s. This experience allowed the young comedian to be fully involved in the vibrant and genuine comedy scene of New York City at that time.

The unrestricted environment drove Jerry to enhance his resilience and project a more assured presence on stage, which proved beneficial for him.

The Comedy Store: Even though he was stationed in New York, Seinfeld often performed at the iconic Comedy Store in Los Angeles during his early career. Mitzi Shore, the owner, mentored Jerry and allowed him to test his jokes nightly alongside other up-and-coming comedians.

Seinfeld's exposure to the diverse club scenes in New York and Los Angeles provided him with different viewpoints that influenced the urban, relatable appeal of his comedy routine.

Jerry Seinfeld

These well-known comedy clubs played a crucial role in shaping Seinfeld's comedic personality by providing guidance and tough critique. The specific atmosphere and viewers in New York greatly influenced his growth as an artist.

2.3 Rise To Prominence

Seinfeld spent years performing in comedy clubs before achieving a breakthrough in 1981 with his debut on The Tonight Show hosted by Johnny Carson. Making an appearance on the show was seen as a significant achievement for aspiring comedians back then.

Seinfeld's successful performance, featuring jokes about Halloween and mall shopping, led to many opportunities. Carson was a well-known fan and frequently invited Jerry back as a regular guest on his show in the 1980s.

Mainstream fame: Jerry Seinfeld's popularity soared after appearing on The Tonight Show. He began making

Jerry Seinfeld

regular appearances on other popular TV shows such as Late Night with David Letterman. In 1987, his first HBO special, "Jerry Seinfeld's Stand-Up Confidential," received high ratings.

Seinfeld became one of the most popular and well-paid comedians on the concert scene by the late 1980s due to his witty observations on everyday details and casual way of speaking. His performances were consistently sold out at arenas nationwide.

NBC offered Seinfeld a sitcom deal in 1988 due to his mainstream success and ability to humorously analyze everyday life. The show, titled "Show About Nothing," debuted in 1989 with mixed reviews but ultimately became a cultural sensation.

Jerry Seinfeld's journey to success in the comedy industry was lengthy, as he spent more than ten years working his way up through the comedy club circuit before finally achieving recognition in the early 1980s. His breakthrough moment came when he made an

Jerry Seinfeld

appearance on The Tonight Show, which rapidly boosted his popularity and established him as one of the top comedy figures of the time.

Jerry Seinfeld

CHAPTER 3: THE SHOW ABOUT NOTHING

Jerry Seinfeld co-created and starred in the iconic sitcom "Seinfeld," which gained the nickname "The Show About Nothing."

The idea for the show originated from an unsuccessful pitch made by Jerry Seinfeld and fellow comedian Larry David to NBC for a sitcom that would explore how a comedian comes up with material. Although NBC rejected the pitch, they recognized the unique comedic style of Seinfeld and encouraged them to create a show based on his humorous observations about everyday life.

The casting and characters of the show include Jerry Seinfeld playing a fictionalized version of himself, alongside Jason Alexander in the role of his best friend George, Julia Louis-Dreyfus as his ex-girlfriend Elaine,

Jerry Seinfeld and Michael Richards as his eccentric neighbor Kramer.

The primary focus of each episode's plot revolved around four characters engaging in casual conversations and embarking on chaotic misadventures triggered by ordinary situations.

Unconventional Style: Seinfeld broke away from traditional sitcom norms right from the beginning with its unique storytelling style that lacked sentimental moments and moral lessons. The deliberately jarring theme music further emphasized its departure from the mainstream. The show's edgy humor, centered around urban life, challenged typical boundaries.

Numerous people appreciated its unique approach to portraying the small details of daily life freshly, especially when compared to other comedies aimed at families during that time. While critics initially criticized it for being too focused on New York City, it soon developed a devoted fan base."

Jerry Seinfeld

Pop Culture Influence: Despite initially modest ratings, Seinfeld gained momentum through word-of-mouth during its nine-season run from 1989 to 1998. The show became a cultural phenomenon by incorporating witty catchphrases such as "No soup for you!".

Today, its influence is still widely recognized, as it has greatly influenced subsequent sitcoms and is frequently mentioned in various forms of media. It is often regarded as one of the most significant and influential television comedies in history.

Seinfeld's unconventional premise was insightful in hindsight as it cleverly mocked societal norms using endearing oddball characters.

3.1 Establishing A Cultural Phenomenon.

Here are some important details about how the television show Seinfeld transitioned from a unique concept to becoming a significant cultural phenomenon.

Jerry Seinfeld

Slow Burn Success: When Seinfeld first aired in 1989, it received average reviews and had modest ratings. Critics didn't quite understand the "show about nothing" idea, finding it too unconventional and specific. Nonetheless, its distinct conversational comedy resonated with a loyal group of fans.

Seinfeld's popularity grew steadily through word-of-mouth promotion, clever writing, and well-developed characters. By the fourth season, it had secured a spot as one of the top 10 TV shows in terms of popularity.

As it reached its peak in the mid-90s, Seinfeld became more than just a television show, becoming a significant element of popular culture. Its unique characters, iconic catchphrases like "No soup for you," and clever social commentary established it as a defining representation of the era.

Jerry Seinfeld

The Contest" episode of the show pushed boundaries with its edgy comedy, becoming a touchstone for a generation due to its clever commentary on relationships, social norms, and everyday life quirks.

Seinfeld's enduring popularity was partly due to its early adoption of product integration and marketing partnerships. The show featured various product placements, such as Snickers in the "Look to the Cookie" episode, and collaborated on advertising campaigns that helped boost its widespread appeal.

After ending in 1998, Seinfeld continued to be popular through reruns, top-selling DVDs, and its impact on future sitcoms such as Curb Your Enthusiasm. It is commonly seen as one of the best and most important comedy shows in TV history."

Initially considered strange, Seinfeld's rapid ascension was a result of a combination of intelligent writing, societal significance, and business acumen. This combination turned the show from just a sitcom into a

Jerry Seinfeld

booming cultural sensation that defined the era of the 1990s.

3.2 Behind The Scenes Of The Iconic Sitcom.

The brilliance of Seinfeld came from its collaborative writers' room, which was overseen by Jerry Seinfeld and Larry David. They promoted a creative process where ideas were generated from casual discussions and ordinary observations were exaggerated to ridiculous levels.

Instead of following typical sitcom formats, they concentrated on fully delving into the absurd logic of each silly premise.
Writers such as Larry Charles also pushed the envelope with edgier episodes like "The Contest."

The Seinfeld team adopted a "no hugging, no learning" approach from the beginning to go against the norm of sitcoms with moral lessons. The characters remained

Jerry Seinfeld

steadfast in their self-centered and trivial behaviors without any sentimental character development.

The decision to do so enabled the comedy to maintain its uncompromising and delightful cynicism towards human behavior, showcasing a daring and freeing creative choice for the writers.

Mythical Setting: The show was meant to portray the gritty atmosphere of recession-era New York City in the early 1990s, but over time, main sets such as Jerry's iconic apartment gained a legendary status."

Every small element, including the couch cushions and the preserved marble rye, was carefully overseen. Seinfeld and his team paid close attention to detail to emphasize the significant concepts of the show.

Even though Seinfeld had well-written scripts, the actors such as Julia Louis-Dreyfus and Jason Alexander had the opportunity to improvise and ad-lib during rehearsals to keep the dialogue natural and spontaneous."

Jerry Seinfeld

Their sharp portrayal of characters and excellent teamwork created numerous memorable moments through the spontaneous development of dialogue during the intensive rehearsal period.

Seinfeld's writer's room had a reputation for pushing boundaries and breaking norms, along with an improvisational approach and an intense focus on details, which all contributed to the show's iconic status.

Jerry Seinfeld

CHAPTER 4: BEYOND SEINFELD

These are some important facts about Jerry Seinfeld's career and activities following the conclusion of the beloved television show Seinfeld in 1998:

Jerry Seinfeld went back to his passion for stand-up comedy after the end of Seinfeld. He started touring regularly and his 1998 tour was a hit, leading to the production of the groundbreaking documentary comedy film Comedian, giving viewers a behind-the-scenes look at his creative process."

Over the years, he has embarked on numerous highly successful stand-up tours around the world, performing in packed arenas. In 2020, he released his first stand-up special on Netflix titled 23 Hours to Kill, marking a return to the genre after almost a quarter-century.

Comedians in Cars Getting Coffee" is a web series created by Seinfeld in 2012 for Crackle/Sony, where

Jerry Seinfeld

Jerry picks up a comedian in a classic car and they go for coffee.

Throughout 11 seasons, the program showcased extensive discussions and highlighted Seinfeld's skills as an interviewer and comedic commentator. It played a pivotal role in paving the way for and establishing credibility for longer digital content.

Seinfeld has continued to work in television production, collaborating on the creation and production of the animated film Bee Movie in 2004. Additionally, he was a producer for the well-received documentary Comedian in 2002.

His first experience directing was with the animated comedy The Bee Movie in 2007. Although the film received a range of reviews, it showcases his ongoing commitment to exploring other creative endeavors outside of acting.

Jerry Seinfeld

Renowned writer Jerry took advantage of his fame by writing numerous successful books throughout his career. Among these are SeinLanguage from 1993, which explores the language of the show, and Is This Anything? released in 2020, focusing on his top performances and memorable moments.

Jerry Seinfeld, who is estimated to have a net worth exceeding $950 million, has successfully moved beyond his role as a sitcom star to take on multiple roles in his post-Seinfeld life. These roles include being a touring standup comedian, producer, director, interviewer, author, and influencer.

4.1 Exploring New Frontiers

Seinfeld was a pioneer in the world of web series when he created and starred in Comedians in Cars Getting Coffee in 2012. This groundbreaking show had a straightforward concept, with Jerry picking up another comedian in a vintage car to grab a coffee and have a chat.

Jerry Seinfeld

The show ran for 11 seasons and 84 episodes on Crackle/Sony, offering detailed interviews and showcasing the comedic creative process. It was a trailblazer in producing longer digital content and encouraged other comedians to start their projects.

The show received praise from critics and allowed Seinfeld to showcase his skills as an interviewer, writer, and producer beyond his usual stand-up comedy.

Jerry Seinfeld made his directorial debut in 2007 with the animated comedy Bee Movie after closely observing the production process on Seinfeld for years. He co-wrote the script, produced the film, and provided the voice for the protagonist bee Barry B. Benson.

Although the movie received a variety of opinions from critics, it allowed Seinfeld to explore a new form of artistic expression in computer animation. The impressive $150 million earnings at the box office

Jerry Seinfeld

demonstrated his enduring popularity with audiences following the end of his sitcom.

After ending his iconic show in 1998, Seinfeld made a strong comeback by returning to his origins as a standup comedian. In the same year, he embarked on a highly successful comedy tour across the country, which was captured in the 2002 film Comedian, offering a transparent glimpse into his creative process.

He has been touring all over the world, performing in large venues with his iconic observational comedy routines. In 2020, he released his first Netflix special in almost 25 years titled 23 Hours to Kill.

Despite attaining immense success in television across generations, Seinfeld continues to venture into new avenues and artistic outlets such as digital content creation, animation, and filmmaking, and revisiting his roots in stand-up comedy to stay relevant and influential in the comedy industry.

Jerry Seinfeld

4.2 Post-seinfeld Projects And Endeavors

Comedian (2002): Seinfeld returned to his standup comedy roots in this documentary film as he embarked on a comeback tour in 1998, following the end of his popular sitcom. Directed by Christian Charles, the film showcased Seinfeld's raw journey of creating and delivering new material after being away from the stage for years. It received praise from critics for offering a revealing glimpse into Seinfeld's creative process.

The 2007 film "Bee Movie" marked Seinfeld's initial venture into animation, where he played a role in writing, producing, and voicing a character in this computer-animated comedy that focused on a bee taking legal action against humans for their exploitation of bees. Despite being a commercial success, the movie received a combination of positive and negative critiques from reviewers. Nevertheless, it provided Seinfeld with the opportunity to showcase his skills in a different aspect of the entertainment industry, as a director, writer, and voice artist.

Jerry Seinfeld

Comedians in Cars Getting Coffee (2012-2019) was a web series created by Seinfeld where he would pick up a fellow comedian in a classic car and have a coffee-fueled conversation. Across 11 seasons and 84 episodes, this show helped elevate the credibility of long-form digital content. Seinfeld's talent as an interviewer and understanding of comedy was on full display in this simple yet effective format."

After finishing his sitcom, Seinfeld took advantage of his popularity by regularly performing stand-up tours. He embarked on significant tours such as the 1998 I'm Telling You for the Last Time, the 2003 The Homeowner, and the 2019-2022 residency at New York's Beacon Theatre. His first Netflix special in almost 25 years was 23 Hours to Kill, released in 2020.

In the years following his iconic sitcom, Seinfeld has tirelessly delved into various creative mediums such as documentaries, animation, and web series to solidify his lasting cultural influence."

Jerry Seinfeld

4.3 Challenges In The World Of Entertainment.

Throughout his entertainment career, Jerry Seinfeld has encountered numerous obstacles despite his immense success and revolutionary influence on comedy.

In the beginning, Seinfeld faced challenges trying to gain recognition, just like many other comedians. He had to work hard at obscure venues and handle disruptions from hecklers in the tough New York comedy scene of the 1970s. It wasn't until he appeared on The Tonight Show in 1981, after facing multiple rejections, that he finally achieved his big break after more than ten years of dedication.

Critical backlash to Seinfeld was significant at first, despite now being considered one of the best sitcoms. Critics initially gave it harsh reviews, rejecting its unusual "show about nothing" concept when it first aired in 1989. There were concerns that its edgy New York humor would not appeal to the wider audience.

Jerry Seinfeld

The creators of Seinfeld often clashed with NBC's standards department due to the show's provocative content and suggestive humor. Episodes like "The Contest," which tackled the topic of masturbation, were frequently subject to censorship battles over what was deemed appropriate.

Concerns about a lack of creativity: With Seinfeld reaching peak popularity in the mid-90s, Seinfeld began to worry about the show's quality and the risk of declining success. These worries led to the decision to end the show on a high note after season 9."

After Seinfeld ended its run in the late 90s, Jerry Seinfeld had to navigate the challenge of breaking free from being typecast solely as a sitcom actor. This resulted in a phase of reevaluation and a return to his stand-up comedy origins, as seen in projects such as the 2002 documentary Comedian.

Jerry Seinfeld

Throughout his entertainment career, Jerry Seinfeld faced numerous challenges, including a lack of initial recognition, censorship limitations, and the need to redefine his image after achieving iconic status in his sitcom. These obstacles constantly pushed him to test his creativity.

4.4 Triumphs In The Entertainment Field

Significant progress on The Tonight Show (1981): Seinfeld had been facing challenges in little-known comedy clubs for years until he finally got his big opportunity with his debut appearance on The Tonight Show Starring Johnny Carson in 1981. The audience loved his performance, which impressed Carson and led to him becoming a key advocate who invited Seinfeld back multiple times. This increased visibility on a popular platform helped boost Seinfeld's career."

The iconic sitcom Seinfeld, co-created and starring Jerry, was born in 1989 and ran until 1998. Despite being initially criticized by critics, it eventually became one of

Jerry Seinfeld

the most influential shows of all time. Its unique comedic style and impact on future series solidified Seinfeld as a trailblazer in comedy.

Seinfeld's brilliance was centered on turning ordinary elements of everyday life into comedic gold, such as wardrobe choices like puffy shirts and food items like marble rye. His talent for uncovering humor in the mundane elevated his observational comedy to become a defining voice of his generation.

Unprecedented Achievement: During the height of his popularity in the '90s sitcom era, Seinfeld was recognized as one of the top comedians globally. He achieved remarkable success with his bestseller SeinLanguage and became one of the highest-earning entertainers thanks to syndication agreements and live performances."

Jerry Seinfeld demonstrated pioneering entrepreneurial skills in the comedy industry, showcasing his ability to cleverly integrate products into his sitcom and create the

Jerry Seinfeld

successful web series, Comedians in Cars Getting Coffee. Through these innovative marketing strategies, Seinfeld has effectively established himself as a prominent comedy brand and creator, ensuring his continued cultural significance.

Jerry Seinfeld's distinct voice and business savvy have propelled him to become a powerhouse in the entertainment industry throughout his 40+ year career, starting from humble beginnings and achieving success with a groundbreaking sitcom, paving the way for new comedic platforms.

Jerry Seinfeld

CHAPTER 5: PERSONAL LIFE

Jerry Seinfeld was born in Brooklyn, New York to Kalman and Betty Seinfeld. His father worked as a sign maker, and his mother was a homemaker. He also has an older sister named Carolyn.

Seinfeld tied the knot with Jessica Sklar in 1999, after meeting her at a Reebok sports club the previous year. They have three children together - a daughter named Sascha (born in 2000) and two sons, Julian Kal (2003) and Shepherd Kellen (2005). The family currently lives in East Hampton, New York.

Jerry had been in several notable relationships before Jessica. He was romantically involved with Shoshanna Lonstein, the inspiration for the character Susan on Seinfeld, from the late 1980s to the early 1990s. Additionally, he was in a four-year relationship with Carol Leifer, who is a writer and comedian.

Jerry Seinfeld

Jerry is very interested in collecting vintage cars and Porsches. He is a devoted automotive enthusiast and even based his Comedians in Cars Getting Coffee series on this hobby. It is believed that his car collection is valued at more than $15 million.

Jerry Seinfeld is actively engaged in philanthropic endeavors, particularly as a part-time professor at his former school Queens College, and advocating for causes centered around childhood education and services.

When Jerry Seinfeld is not busy touring, writing, acting, or collecting cars, he leads a private life in the Hamptons with his wife Jessica, and children. His journey to achieving personal happiness reflects the challenges and successes he has experienced throughout his iconic comedy career.

Jerry Seinfeld

5.1 Personal Milestones

Jerry Seinfeld has experienced various important events in his personal life, all of which have added to the unique fabric of his journey.

1. Jerry Seinfeld tied the knot with Jessica Sklar in 1999, a significant event in his personal life. Their marriage has brought Seinfeld joy and stability, as Sklar serves as a supportive partner and they have a loving family together.

2. Seinfeld has found fatherhood to be a profoundly impactful experience that has greatly changed him. The arrival of his three children has brought him immense joy and a sense of completeness, altering the way he views his priorities and life in general.

3. Achievements in Seinfeld's Career: Seinfeld has reached many significant milestones in his career, from the popularity of his TV show to the praise he received for his stand-up performances and other projects in the

Jerry Seinfeld

entertainment industry. These accomplishments have cemented his reputation as a highly influential figure in comedy."

4. Charitable Efforts: Seinfeld has always been dedicated to philanthropy, showing consistent support for different causes and organizations. His donations to education, environmental protection, and medical studies demonstrate his dedication to creating a positive influence outside of the entertainment industry.

5. Legacy and Influence: Seinfeld's impact goes beyond his achievements, as he is considered a cultural icon. His contribution to comedy and mainstream culture has been significant, serving as an inspiration for many comedians and performers to emulate his success.

These individual achievements not only highlight various aspects of Jerry Seinfeld's life but also emphasize the complexity of his personality and the lasting impact he has made in both his professional and personal life."

Jerry Seinfeld

5.2 Managing the balance between public recognition and personal space.

Balancing between fame and privacy has always been a struggle for Jerry Seinfeld during his career. Being a highly visible figure in the entertainment industry, he has had to deal with constant public scrutiny while also protecting his personal life and boundaries.

Seinfeld has consistently safeguarded his privacy by choosing to keep his personal life away from public attention. Despite being famous, he leads a modest lifestyle, steering clear of the typical behaviors associated with celebrity status and striving to maintain a sense of normality in his everyday interactions."

Seinfeld maintains a careful balance by keeping his public persona separate from his private life. Although he is open and engaging in public appearances and interviews, he is cautious not to reveal too much about his personal life. This ensures that certain parts of his

Jerry Seinfeld

life are kept private and away from media and public scrutiny.

Seinfeld is famous for his clever and modest humor, frequently employing comedy as a defense mechanism to avoid personal questions and control his own story. Through his use of humor and cleverness, he successfully deals with the challenges of being famous with elegance and genuineness, staying genuine to himself while protecting his personal life."

Jerry Seinfeld's skill in managing his fame and privacy is attributed to his strong dedication to being authentic and preserving his true self. He has managed to create a balance by establishing clear limits and remaining faithful to his beliefs, which has allowed him to maintain a public presence while protecting the privacy of his personal life.

Jerry Seinfeld

CHAPTER 6: LEGACY

Jerry Seinfeld's lasting influence on comedy and popular culture is deeply ingrained, surpassing generations. He changed television with his innovative show "Seinfeld," which set a new standard in the genre and resonated with audiences globally.

Several important aspects define Seinfeld's lasting impact.

1. New kind of comedy: "Seinfeld" brought in a fresh approach to comedy, famously known as "a show about nothing. The sitcom grasped the spirit of the 1990s and altered the television industry with its sharp writing, clever plots, and relatable characters.

2. Long-lasting Impact: The impact of Seinfeld on the comedy industry extends far and wide, motivating numerous comedians and TV producers to mimic his unique style and perspective. His signature

Jerry Seinfeld

observational humor and ability to find humor in the small details of everyday life have become defining characteristics of modern comedy.

3. Cultural Significance: "Seinfeld" continues to be a cultural phenomenon, with its popular phrases, characters, and unforgettable scenes deeply embedded in the public consciousness long after it ended. The show's influence goes beyond just entertainment, playing a role in shaping societal beliefs and impacting discussions on various subjects like relationships and social norms.

4. Jerry Seinfeld has achieved ongoing success in stand-up comedy, television, and other creative ventures even after "Seinfeld." His capacity to adapt to changing trends while remaining authentic to his comedic origins has cemented his reputation as a comedy icon.

5. Seinfeld's lasting impact includes his charitable activities and advocacy work. He has backed several charitable organizations, focusing on education, environmental protection, and health research,

Jerry Seinfeld

leveraging his influence to bring about positive change in the world outside of the entertainment industry.

Jerry Seinfeld has been known for his innovation, influence, and lasting significance. His remarkable contributions to comedy and entertainment have made a lasting impact on the cultural scene, guaranteeing that his legacy will remain influential for years to come.

6.1 Impact On Comedy

Jerry Seinfeld's influence on the world of comedy cannot be overstated, as his impact is felt in stand-up clubs, TV studios, and comedy stages globally. Below are some of how Seinfeld has changed the comedy scene:

1. Seinfeld is well-known for his skill in observational humor, which involves closely observing the peculiarities and nonsense of everyday life. His talent for finding humor in ordinary situations has influenced many comedians to delve into the same comedic theme,

Jerry Seinfeld

resulting in a rise of observational comedy in both stand-up acts and television shows.

2. The impact of the sitcom "Seinfeld" was significant, as it revolutionized the genre by focusing on ordinary situations and everyday dialogues instead of conventional storylines. This fresh storytelling style and its bold exploration of controversial topics set the stage for a wave of innovative television comedy that took inspiration from it.

3. Cultural Influence: "Seinfeld" not only amused viewers but also mirrored and molded cultural beliefs and customs. The program's famous phrases, remarkable characters, and memorable scenes have become deeply embedded in mainstream culture, impacting everything from clothing styles to social manners.

4. Stand-up comedy experienced a resurgence in the 1990s, with Jerry Seinfeld's success on "Seinfeld" playing a significant role. His fame and appeal played a

Jerry Seinfeld

key part in bringing stand-up comedy back into the spotlight and influencing a fresh wave of aspiring comedians to enter the field.

5. Taking Comedy to a Higher Level: Seinfeld's careful focus on the little things and his strong work ethic have raised comedy to a higher level as an art form. His drive for perfection and his constant search for the ideal punchline have established a significant benchmark for comedians worldwide, motivating them to explore new possibilities in comedy.

Jerry Seinfeld has had a broad and lasting influence on the world of comedy. His groundbreaking sitcom, original stand-up performances, and significant impact on popular culture have solidified his reputation as one of the most influential comedians in history.

Jerry Seinfeld

6.2 Influence On Modern-day Comedians

Jerry Seinfeld has had a significant impact on modern-day comedians, molding the world of comedy in various ways.

1. The comedian Seinfeld is known for his expertise in observational comedy, which has greatly influenced modern comedians. Numerous comedians are inspired by Seinfeld's talent for finding humor in the small details of daily life, and they incorporate observational elements into their performances.

2. Seinfeld showed that humor can be found in ordinary subjects. His openness to address everyday topics, such as waiting in line at the bank and the complexities of relationships, has inspired modern comedians to delve into similar themes, highlighting the ridiculousness of everyday life in their jokes.

3. Focus on Skill: Seinfeld's careful focus on detail and his dedication to his work are seen as an example for

Jerry Seinfeld

comedians who are trying to make it in the industry. His determination to improve jokes, sharpen comedic timing, and master delivery has motivated many comedians to emphasize skill and quality in their comedy endeavors.

4. Creative way of telling stories: "Seinfeld" changed the way sitcom stories are told by introducing a fresh narrative structure and character-focused humor. Modern comedians have been inspired by Seinfeld's unique storytelling style, trying out non-linear stories, diverse casts, and unusual plots in their comedy works.

5. Handling Celebrity Status: Seinfeld, a famous figure who prioritizes personal privacy, has had a significant impact on modern comedians dealing with issues related to fame. His skill in managing public exposure while maintaining personal limits sets an example for comedians navigating the difficulties of fame in today's digital era.

Jerry Seinfeld

Jerry Seinfeld has had a diverse impact on modern comedians, including his unique comedic style, storytelling approach, dedication to excellence, and handling of fame. His lasting influence is evident in the continued inspiration he provides to comedians globally, guaranteeing that his mark on the comedy world will last for many years to come.

6.3 Long-lasting Popularity And Significance In Culture

Jerry Seinfeld remains popular and culturally significant because he can connect with audiences of all ages and has left a lasting impression on different areas of popular culture.

1. Seinfeld's comedic style is considered timeless as it can resonate with audiences regardless of the era or culture.
His jokes and insights on various topics like daily life, personal connections, and societal conventions continue to be pertinent and relatable to people of all generations.

Jerry Seinfeld

This lasting appeal of Seinfeld's humor plays a significant role in the continued success and popularity of his comedic work.

2. The classic television series "Seinfeld" remains well-loved and popular, even many years after it first premiered. Its enduring humor, beloved characters, and memorable lines have established it as a cultural icon, with younger audiences still finding and enjoying its genius."

3. The syndication and streaming of "Seinfeld" has exposed the show to new viewers globally, making it popular among both old and new fans, thus sustaining its cultural significance over time.

4. Jerry Seinfeld's impact on comedy goes beyond just "Seinfeld." His stand-up shows, interviews, and other comedic projects remain popular with audiences and motivate up-and-coming comedians. His comedic legacy is a source of inspiration for the comedy world, ensuring that he remains culturally significant.

Jerry Seinfeld

5. Seinfeld's influence on popular culture goes beyond comedy, with his catchphrases, memorable scenes, and iconic characters becoming ingrained in mainstream culture. This has affected everything from fashion trends to societal expectations. His imprint on popular culture is unquestionable, guaranteeing his enduring significance in the cultural landscape.

Jerry Seinfeld's lasting fame and significance in society are a result of his classic humor, iconic TV series, availability on syndication and streaming platforms, comedic heritage, and enduring influence on popular culture. As a comedic legend, he still entertains and motivates viewers globally, solidifying his place as a cultural icon.

CONCLUSION

When we explore the "Jerry Seinfeld Biography: A Life in Laughter," we see the remarkable story of a highly influential comedian who has left a lasting mark on the world of entertainment. Starting from his modest origins in Brooklyn to reaching immense success on television, Jerry Seinfeld's life demonstrates the profound ability of humor to change lives.

As we finish reading this fascinating biography, we are reminded of Seinfeld's lasting impact on comedy and popular culture. With his insightful observations, sharp humor, and commitment to his work, he has transformed the comedy scene, influencing many comedians and delighting audiences worldwide.

However, beneath the surface of joy and approval, there is a more profound reality. It is the tale of a man who has successfully managed the challenges of being famous with humility, elegance, and an unwavering

Jerry Seinfeld

dedication to staying true to himself. Seinfeld's consistent adherence to his beliefs, his unwavering loyalty to his loved ones, and his endless enthusiasm for comedy act as a source of motivation for everyone.

As we say goodbye to the book "Jerry Seinfeld: A Life in Laughter," we are filled with a deep admiration for the person who brings laughter - a person whose comedy talent is endless, whose influence is immeasurable, and whose memory will last for many years to come."

Jerry Seinfeld's life demonstrates the lasting impact of humor, serving as a reminder that even amid life's challenges and unknowns, there is always space for happiness, wit, and clever jokes. As we finish reading this extraordinary biography, we do so with gratitude for the joy that Jerry Seinfeld has provided us and a desire to continue his comedic tradition in the years to come.